Amelia Earhart

Flying into Adventure

Tamara Hollingsworth

Consultant

Glenn Manns, M.A.
Teaching American History Coordinator
Ohio Valley Educational Cooperative

Publishing Credits

Dona Herweck Rice, *Editor-in-Chief*; Lee Aucoin, *Creative Director*; Conni Medina, M.A.Ed., *Editorial Director*; Jamey Acosta, *Associate Editor*; Neri Garcia, *Senior Designer*; Stephanie Reid, *Photo Researcher*; Rachelle Cracchiolo, M.A.Ed., *Publisher*

Image Credits

Teacher Created Materials

5301 Oceanus Drive
Huntington Beach, CA 92649-1030
http://www.tcmpub.com
ISBN 978-1-4333-1595-4
©2011 Teacher Created Materials, Inc.
Printed in China

Table of Contents

Meet Amelia

Amelia Earhart was a **brave** woman. She loved flying. When she lived, many people thought women were not smart enough to fly. Amelia did not care what people thought. She did what she loved.

Amelia's airplane lands on water.

Fun Fact

Amelia was the first woman to fly to faraway places all by herself.

Being Herself

Amelia was born in Kansas on July 24, 1897. She loved to play outside and get dirty. Back then, little girls always wore dresses. But Amelia's mother let her wear **bloomers** when she played outside.

Amelia's childhood home

Bloomers are a type of ruffled pants worn under skirts and dresses.

Amelia and her younger sister, Muriel

Amelia saw her first airplane when she was 10. She did not like it. She thought it was loud and ugly. She was more interested in science. At school, Amelia loved her science classes best.

An old airplane at an airshow in 1908

Fun Fact

Amelia went to six different high schools.

Flying High

One day Amelia and her friend went to a **stunt** show. Airplanes did tricks up in the sky. Amelia saw an airplane swoop out of the air and zoom near her. She said she heard the airplane calling to her. Soon she took flying lessons.

A woman standing on an airplane during a stunt show

Fun Fact

Most people did not think that women could fly airplanes. But as a child, Amelia wanted to learn how to fly. As an adult, she taught people how to fly.

Amelia standing in front of an airplane

People said Amelia was crazy for trying to fly. But she loved her flying lessons. She began saving her money. She had her eye on a little yellow airplane. It took six months of saving. Amelia bought the yellow airplane and called it *Canary*.

Amelia's yellow airplane *Canary*

Amelia used *Canary* to set her first record. She flew 14,000 feet into the sky!

Amelia's airplane was yellow like a canary.

Record Setter

People heard about Amelia's love of flying. One day a man asked if she wanted to be the first woman to fly across the Atlantic Ocean. Of course she did! Amelia was excited to ride along. In 1928, she became the first woman to fly across the Atlantic Ocean as a **passenger**.

Friendship, the airplane Amelia flew in across the Atlantic Ocean

Fun Fact

Amelia wrote *20 Hours, 40 Minutes: Our Flight in the* Friendship. The book was about her trip as a passenger across the Atlantic Ocean.

Amelia standing in front of her airplane, *Friendship*

Fun Fact

Amelia became famous.
Women wanted to
be like her. Amelia
designed her own line
of clothing for them.

Amelia in one of the dresses she designed

A man named George Putnam had helped plan Amelia's flight across the Atlantic. Soon after, George and Amelia fell in love. But Amelia did not want to get married. She thought that meant she had to quit flying. George said she should keep doing what she loved. The couple married on February 7, 1931.

Fun Fact

Many wives take their husband's last name. Not Amelia! She kept her own last name.

Solo Flight

Amelia and George planned a **solo** trip for Amelia. She would fly alone across the Atlantic Ocean. No woman had ever flown that far before. Many people said a woman could not do it. But Amelia had her mind set that she could do it.

Amelia and George looking at a globe and planning her world flight

Amelia posing with her foot propped up on her airplane

In May 1932, Amelia began her solo flight. She was headed for Paris. But strong winds made it hard to fly. Amelia had to land sooner than she planned. She landed on a farm in Ireland. She had made it across the Atlantic Ocean alone!

Amelia shares her route over the Atlantic Ocean with the news.

Fun Fact

President Herbert Hoover gave Amelia a special medal for her flight.

Last Flight

Amelia wanted to be the first woman to fly around the world. In 1937, she and her friend Fred Noonan began the trip. They made it almost all the way around the world. They had to land on an island to **refuel** the airplane.

Amelia, Fred, and friends standing in front of her airplane

Amelia and Fred's whole trip was 29,000 miles. They had only 7,000 miles left.

Amelia sits under a map showing her route around the world.

No woman had ever tried to fly as far as Amelia did. Many people were inspired by her courage.

Fred and Amelia

Amelia and Fred took off again. They were headed to a tiny island called Howland Island. The weather was bad. The winds were strong. The airplane never made it to the island. People searched for Amelia and Fred for years. But they were never found.

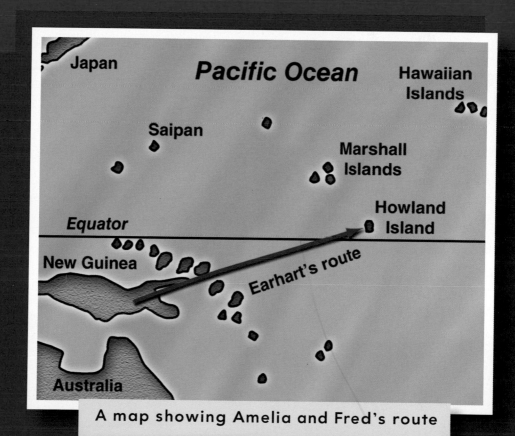

A map showing Amelia and Fred's route

Amelia's Example

Amelia believed in herself. She knew she was strong, smart, and brave. She did not listen when people said she could not do something. She proved that women could do the things men did. This is why people still admire her today.

Fun Fact

Amelia was different from many women in her time. She followed her own path.

Amelia in the cockpit of her airplane

1897

Amelia Earhart is born in Kansas.

1921

Amelia buys *Canary.*

1931

Amelia and George Putnam get married.

Line

1932

Amelia flies alone across the Atlantic Ocean.

1937

Amelia tries to fly around the world.

Glossary

bloomers—ruffled pants that are worn under skirts and dresses

brave—not afraid

passenger—someone who rides in a car, bus, or plane, but does not drive it

refuel—to get more fuel or gasoline

solo—done alone, without anyone else helping you

stunt—a daring and dangerous performance

Index

Americans Today

Stacy Allison was the first American woman to climb to the top of Mt. Everest. The height and weather made this very hard to do. Mt. Everest is the tallest mountain in the world. The first time Stacy tried, she did not make it. But she tried again. And she did it!